DragonSito Publishing
11317 SW. 111 St.
Miami, FL 33176

www.dragonsitopublishing.c‌⸱...

Ordering Information: Quantity sales. Special discounts are available on quantity purchases by corporations, associations, and others. For details, contact the publisher at the address above. Orders by U.S. trade bookstores and wholesalers. Please contact Lightning Source: Tel: (615) 213-5815; Fax: (615) 213-4725 or visit www.lightningsource.com.

Cover Art Design - Marie-Elena Joseph & Anthony Beyrle
Illustrations – Victoria Caffin
Forward – Patrick Joseph Brown

Printed in the United States of America

In Memory of Michael Garcia,
My Grandfather.

I was both exhilarated and honoured to write the four-word or more to the works of this new and ageless poet.

Most of you will know an "Elfin" if you had the chance to meet one, if not, a definition may suffice.

A definition then – suggestive of an Elf – made; done; produced by an Elf – small and sprightly – having a magical quality or charm – fairylike.

These qualities are what makes these poems so special, and the Elfin qualities of Joshua so connected to the Universe of mind, body, and spirit that graciously weaves its meandering threads of thoughts throughout his works.

I recommend "We Were Born Before," "A More Than Lovely Place," and "Elfin Mathematics," however, you will find your own joy of enjoyment as this new and exciting Poet enters your thoughts and you have your own reflections.

So sit back, relax, and enjoy Elfin.

- Patrick J. Brown

TABLE OF CONTENT

A Festival of Rats

Heaven opened, and the heavy rains fell,
as some talked that jibber jabber;
that late-night campfire swagger,
others, with their long days' traveled,
came to hear the professor boil and toil.

With his glasses golden and rimmed,
time took upon a magnified deconstruction.
Space stood still. And from the dust,
with the alchemist's precise measurements,
blew through the winds an electrostatic shock,
painting life's elements and filling in the lines.

From the shadows of the oak tree's rooted bowels
purred a sharp Persian cat,
as a family of rats shared a joyful dance
up 'top the earth's mushroom caps.
The Queen Mother wore her smile,
as her children laughed
and were happy for a while.

Gone and Fishing

with every step taken
'round the puddled water
heavy droplets rise
reaching for the sun
and my feet keep on steppin'
towards a brook of beating tails
a salmon jig of fun
and 'round the worms & hooks
the winded leaves did land
over this school of fish
'curred a muddy water dance

What Sound Will The Rivers Make When They Stop Flowing?

while the earth spun its final spin
the souls of the elders finally did sit
a baby's breath did warm the air
with no price to pay but death

his father and his mother wept
for fear the darkness would never let
yet from the caves blew wind and rain
a pain that brought a child no name

known by the stars and to the earth
as the childish heart that
did, will, and shall forever burn

Something Happened

all is seen and sawed.
freedom birds are caged.
enemies of grey and shade.
a truth is born from ball and chain.
skies are broken with a spearing fire.
minds are jarred and walking wires.

Needlepoint

broken chimes ring heavy
their blackened metal sweetens eyes
and the essence of the night rests
on the sharpened point of a tired needle
above a pentagram of desires

Secondhand Ancestral Tune

the oil's run dry
gears brittle and bruised
time becomes Time's
and the breaks become grooves
all while the mind clicks
to the oldest of tunes
in this clockwork of minds
plays the hand-me-down blues

Queen Victoria

she stood still
weeping over wood and string
that which laid dormant and undone
was resurrected as she sung
and the world was born from the start
with her lips
to the end
with her kiss

smiled today
felt the earth shake
saw life displayed
in a honey-combed state
upon a translucent slate
it came in a whisper
a beaming echo's break
and from its shards
came through the years
a bittersweet chapter
to ungrateful ears

A Finished City

graffiti bleeds with rain from the alleyway
as the poor bathe in new textures
possessed with every gesture
each letter seeps

Electric Polarity

red and blue
thin electrical lines
separate the jesters from fools

within these inherent marks of old
one finds the makings of a hero
a conversion of water to gold

Elfin Mathematics

she sat there,
alone in the corner.
understanding left her gleaming.
her ears, although pointed, gave her alerted beauty,
all as she made sense of the numbers.
never speaking,
her eyes never creeping,
just the words of her silence
and the music of her thoughts.

Departure: Louisiana
Arrival: Miami

Awakening to find myself in a crowded bus.
Slouched and lethargic, I study the passengers.
The bus is moving stealthily as I catch a glimpse
of the black beauty sitting three rows down from the space
between
the window where my head rests and the long leather-
walled tunnel leading to the front of the bus.
The homeless woman, wrapped in rags, turns slowly.
We glance at one another and a tear slips down her face.

::Blinking::

Where was I just now?
How do I go back?

I want to be with her while she cries.
I want to hold her when she dies.

The Birth of the Bohemian Bastard

The café's many refined guests main-line home blends.
"It not being anyone's cup of tea
is what makes It everyone's cup of tea,"
the hag muttered.

Locked in a neighboring table's voice alterations,
my study of a mother breastfeeding begins,
as waiters become tailors,
and fit suits for the bastard's father.

When a Step is Mis-taken

bending and weaving
went the bristles of her brooms
sweeping the stairs of their dirt

beware of spider-lane
where there are iron bars that cage
the road from the seeker
kept by none other than the gate keeper

twirling her rusted keys
'round her yellowed fingers,
with a nose for death and a stink of life,
she turned to me
and stole my mind

Granular and Off-Course

golf courses fizz with bubbles
bringing green to the day's grey troubles
and with a driver at hand
the ball is shot furthest
from the hole where it all began

now I'm stuck in Time's sands
learning with each grain
how to putt with the other hand

ringed courses of ducks in place of horses
spun
and suddenly you've been driven by forces
to dizzily chase pastel trees
a playground of woven steel beams
holding space for any case
of weeping stoners
torn from life's endless seems

and with one stitch left
loosely wound by metallic embrace
the night's shaded clown
a polygraph Judas
prince of deceit
in our own circle
a monkey bar's reach
lies a land of painted clovers,
elementary arts, handicap swings,
and praline rainbow farts

There are Too Many Names to Enter Here

Your eyes are shattered windows
in a world of cold drafts.

You wake to sleep,
'cuz life for you is a joker fresh out of laughs.

Jugglin' your heart and mind with knives and sticks,
your destiny is left cracking like a cat o' nine whip.

With but one step you've left the circus in a Samba,
ready to lance.

Love,
my vorpal sword is sharpened,
and I have for eternity awaited this dance.

Drip Drop Rorschach

as the history of the world
is broken down into molecules
all i could wear to the occasion was a smile
because in its construction there was no me
and in its deconstruction there was no you

so let's get on with the hustle
take off with the silence
say hello to the kindness
and bid farewell to the violence

because in this chemical brew
stands in the way nothing but you
a symbiotic alphabetic occurrence
m comma e both before u

let the illogicals play
there's nothing else to do
but dance with the skeletons
and do as they do
boogie with the elephants
no one's locked up the zoo

so say say
do do
there ain't
there is
nothing and everything
but a me that remarkably reflects you

Land of Fadeless Dreams

As I gazed toward the sky,
my forehead split into a melody
where children sang smiles,
and broken wings were mended,
where rivers flew into hawks,
and the earth's colors blended.

Heavenly shades of homely lullabies
unraveled in a garden of bones,
where seedless souls were planted
beneath the fields of Saint Rose.

Easy strides, brothers and sisters,
tread lightly on these high times
filled with crowded boulevards of
tongues unbeknownst to sand and
unspoken rhyme.

Let not your path be lost in
the easy tunes of growing shadows,
where cold winds win stories,
and all of life's roads are narrow.

How I loved you and will never let you go.

I hadn't touched her in ages,
her body over the years had worn cold,
and the words she'd once spoken with conviction,
were now dust in the torn pages of old.

Where there was once a hole in her room
tunneled to mine through one outstretching shadow,
there is now webs and bones;
memories having long since shattered.

A childish love bred of innocence,
broken by me alone.
With my last final breaths I grasp
for one final word,
one final poem.

A More Than Lovely Place

Cross-legged and smiling,
a bleeding heart of gold,
and in his lap sang a bowl of crystals,
vibrating and shattering
the hotel's young and old.

From the lobby came a howl,
fingers of light and hands to hold.

She Saw My Sins Through Eyes that Sang

A piano wire noose hung
down white walls splashed with color,
where seventeen were dead and buried
beneath pool halls of graffiti memories
and littered cigarette butts.
Hungry puppets were cast
amidst the bamboo & barbwire,
where an African princess sat
swaying with a bottle in hand,
yelling that she had had a
handle on things.

The Devil's Ballad

> *See, it didn't start with the serpent,*
> *it started with me.*
> *My love had returned,*
> *not to dust, but to bone.*

His smile ran off as he walked through the forest,
hearing a tune only the devil could play.

The fruits on the tree were ripe, but never fell,
and the music, however rotten, was sweet.

Ace of Spades

Take a long look at me—
Most of you know I'm dying.
The years we've spent laughing,
and the ones we've spent crying,
have all passed us by. Tonight,
as I walk the house of stairs,
please don't be sad. I will,
and have, always been your Joker,
your King of Clubs,
a jack of swirling diamonds,
a queen of riddled hearts.

Anointed Ones

I

I was told she would come
as a servant with a candle in the night,
bearing eternity beneath her breasts.
And before the darkness she will stand
as a lion with a phoenix for a heart.

While looking into her eyes
her inverted presence will be seen
reflected above the crown of her head,
and for just a moment,
known friends will have turned to smoke.

Thinking it smart to breath,
they will be gone,
returning only in a sigh.

II

You will recognize him by the mark he bears,
his teeth will have no shine,
and the clothes he wears will batter in the wind,
and their rips will tear your mind.

Although his words will make no sense,
and his actions will prove weak and untrue,
the magic that gleams from above his head,
will cower you to your knees – the presence of truth.

Your mother spoke, when you were a child,
of heaven, hell, and all of God's works,
but in your heart you have always known
that your spirit carries the only naked truth.

III

It is with you,
Wisdom has told,
that with nothing said and nothing done,
the world spoils to waste, and haste proves nothing to none.

Remove your lips from the breasts of death,
your nose from the smell of rancid perfume,
and walk into heaven a child of God,
free of the church and their holiday tunes.

When the ball breaks and the earth spins through,
your thoughts and its precepts will shatter you too.
You say you love, but you cast your spells
and break the hearts you choose,

but once the ball breaks and the earth spins through,
you will see that there were none good nor bad,
just a you that sees through you.

Rise with the Mass

drop a clue or take a hint,
the world is ending and
my mind's eye is stretching with every inch.
and so when they call you "antichrist,"
they will remember you by name,
and when they call you "son of god,"
they badger all your claims.
when the light comes shining forth,
dare not you hide beneath the rain,
because the true hell is behind a door
not seen nor touched by man;
it's labeled *"fear"*
with rose decor,
skin-toned with earthy wood.
this door, it whispers
to young and old,
"beware of tapered rears."

there is but one path to follow,
but one to catch flight.
beware my friend, that on this path,
all face their flees and fights.

Bob Dylan

woke up from a nap today with knowledge.
wrote in children's poetics, but i was scotch-drunk.
messaged everyone i knew, but found no companions.
thought of everyone i knew, but loved all of them the same.

where was the art that wounded?
where was the melody that spoke?

my best friend lay in the guest room,
while oscar wilde
sucked,
and there was a band i'd listened to,
that 'sang about diamonds in the rough.
when i read this, i will have sobered from my venture,
my best friend's sister will have dissociated herself,
and the girls i loved will have grown up.

dizzy and tired, words devolve;
products of schooling.
the migraines, in smoke, have found their resolve
beneath
the grasp of rat traps and the sounds of drowned silence.

i remember the crowing night grew old.
that the bar had a candle that went out at each end.
that women i'd learned to love were.
all this, as i held a drink in my mouth,
savoring whatever burn might still be.

Birthright

patients is born
on a table
and the changing lives and times
are spinning and falling
rising and growing
into this
that
and everything fat

aristocratic jacuzzis
full of champagne and elegant pride
scuzzy-bottomed and disgusting
the world rotating around
cuffs and slaves
and shoeshine pay

We were born before.
Don't you remember?

There was a blanket.
and the wind had settled.
Darkness was but a memory
not yet imagined.

The pages, a water paper texture;
history's architecture.

A Place Harder Than a Rock

it occurred to me this morning,
that i'm in a corner of sorts.
lost between angles.
stuck between one choice
or the other.

resolution? a break?
can i add to the mosaic
when questions have stolen my tools?

sitting back and watching,
my hands call for work,
and yet make no movements.

A Portrait of New York times - Rembrandt's Ghost of Men

There was a song playing from the center of the park
to the tune of a spinning carousel;
something from the 1940's.

I remember there were boys dreaming
together, laying on a torn cardboard box,
their dreams spinning too.

They dreamt of a night where two lost souls would
find themselves across the street,
watching from afar,

students at a trapeze school.
I wonder, if Rembrandt were still alive,
would he draw our pets or us,
their owners?

Sleeping Seeds of Days

secrets left amazed
and the sleeping seeds of days
are opened and tolled

ears are bent to listen
to the perilous flight of parables unfolding
time beholding
prophets blinded and dreaming

my own dreams
silence and then applause
a string quartet; *clair de lune*
a buzz
a gimmick
a time set set time and tune

the burning smells of sage and flowers
and i knew that your goodbye
was an unspoken "hello"

i was having a high time
barefoot and turning
thoughts to prayers
a muddy wheel spun and learning

tears bring trouble
tomorrow and rain
a blooming of hard wonders
a looming crane

DragonSito Publishing
-Member Manager-

~o~

Elfin Faolan Chronicles
Author, Editor, Publisher

CPSIA information can be obtained at www.ICGtesting.com
Printed in the USA
LVOW081606300513

336062LV00001BA/1/P